WHERE EAGLES GATHER

WHERE EAGLES GATHER

THE STORY OF THE ALASKA CHILKAT BALD EAGLE PRESERVE

Haines, Alaska

JOE ORDÓÑEZ

This book is dedicated to the memory of my friend Norm Blank,

whose positive presence promoted a pure and healthy Chilkat Valley.

FRONT COVER *Two eagles lock talons in a battle over a fish. The eagle on the bottom was eating the fish. When the other eagle approached, the eagle on the fish flipped over and reached out to fend off the attack.*

PREVIOUS PAGE *Fog and clouds lift off the Chilkat Summit, exposing the peaks and valleys of the Klehini and Kelsall Rivers' headwaters.*

OPPOSITE *Fall colors enliven views from Mosquito Lake State Park and Campground, located in the preserve. Large numbers of black cottonwood, birch, and other hardwood trees give Haines and the preserve some of the best fall foliage in the State of Alaska.*

INSIDE BACK COVER *Northern lights brighten up the sky above Swan View Cabin in the preserve.*

BACK COVER *With wings flared and talons forward, an eagle prepares for a landing.*

The Takhinsha Mountains provide a stunning backdrop to a bald eagle in flight in the Bald Eagle Preserve Council Grounds.

THE FUTURE *of the* EAGLES

Senator Gary Hart

Lupines, members of the pea family, grace the gravel bars along rivers in the preserve. These plants have the ability to colonize areas where soil is low in nitrogen.

A phrase usually used to describe rare political leaders—"charismatic"—is sometimes applied to extraordinary animals. Lions are often described as charismatic. And in the world of birds, few would dispute the use of the word to describe the American bald eagle.

The largest congregation of bald eagles in the world occurs outside Haines, Alaska, where every November upwards of 3,600 of the magnificent creatures feed on salmon run from the Chilkat and Chilkoot Rivers. The area is the 48,000-acre Alaska Chilkat Bald Eagle Preserve, and the author of this book, Joe Ordóñez, knows as much about the preserve and the eagles drawn to it as anyone around.

Though not native to Alaska, I grew up enthralled by pictures and films of the bald eagle. And in 1979 and 1980, as a United States Senator representing the State of Colorado, I participated in the passage of the Alaska National Interest Lands Conservation Act that set aside more than 100 million acres of unspoiled Alaska lands in the National Park system and National Wildlife Preserve system. As one of the principal sponsors of this legislation in the Senate and an active participant in the debate leading up to its successful passage, my greatest focus was on the Chilkat area and the preservation of a national bald eagle sanctuary.

In the hotly contested struggle leading to the final passage of the Act in November 1980, a comprehensive compromise with State of Alaska interests led to the Alaska Chilkat Bald Eagle Preserve being protected by the State of Alaska and therefore excluded from the areas to be protected by the United States government.

After years of hoping one day to get to Haines and see the preserve, the opportunity arose in 2010 when my wife, Lee, and I started a tour of Alaska's Inside Passage by going to Haines to see the Alaska Chilkat Bald Eagle Preserve. Those who have had the opportunity to visit extraordinary areas of the world with an expert guide know the characteristics he or she must possess: knowledge of the area; knowledge of the creatures of the land, water, and air to be seen; and a love of the natural habitat. Joe Ordóñez possesses all these qualities and more—he is a world-class photographer—and it is

difficult to imagine experiencing the Chilkat region without his companionship.

As this brief but comprehensive work demonstrates, Joe has that almost spiritual relationship with nature required of those who want to introduce it to others but, even more importantly, preserve it for our children and future generations. The forces of development, and too often exploitation, have countless promoters on their payrolls. The more humble cohort of preservationists conducts their mission out of reverence for nature, not out of desire for money.

Once again, the Chilkat River watershed is under pressure from proposed mining, the kind of development that could quickly and easily deny the great eagles their unique place of assembly. There are many places to build highways and procure minerals. Other unique places for the great eagles to collect each year may not exist.

There are countless arenas where we will determine whether irreplaceable nature and nature's wildlife or the consumer culture will prevail in the twenty-first century. The Alaska Chilkat Bald Eagle Preserve is at the top of the list. And the eagles are supremely fortunate to have Joe Ordóñez on their side.

—Gary Hart

ABOVE *The contrasting white and dark plumage of the bald eagle is unmistakable.*

OPPOSITE *The setting moon silhouettes an eagle as the sun rises on a crisp November morning in the Bald Eagle Preserve Council Grounds.*

RIGHT *Two trumpeter swans and a merganser float beneath the fog on the Chilkat River.*

ABOVE *Freeze-thaw cycles are typical in the fall in the Chilkat Valley, leading to scenes like this one of ice, water, clouds, and mountains.*

OPPOSITE *As the sun breaks the horizon, the ice closes in on a last remaining section of open water along the river's shore.*

ABOVE LEFT *The red branches of the red-osier dogwood are encased in ice during the first big freeze of the year along Chilkat Inlet.*

ABOVE RIGHT *The rose hip, fruit of the wild rose, forms after the fragrant petals of the flowers have dropped off. This fruit is high in Vitamin C and is best harvested after the first frost.*

RIGHT *Hoarfrost crystals incrementally increase in size during extended periods of cold weather. This crystal formed on the tip of an alder bud.*

OPPOSITE *The first signs of winter are apparent as they come to Mosquito Lake: snow down to the lake level, and the start of lake ice.*

THE ALASKA CHILKAT BALD EAGLE PRESERVE

■ Alaska Chilkat Bald Eagle Preserve

CANADA · UNITED STATES · CANADA

Kelsall River

Chilkat River

Klehini River

Constantine Mine

Klukwan

Skagway

Chilkoot Lake

Chilkat Lake

Chilkat River

Tsirku River

7

Haines

ALASKA

Pyramid Island

Chilkat Mountains

Chilkoot Mountains

Lynn Canal

Anchorage

Area

N

| 0 | | | | | 20 Kilometers |
| 0 | | | | | 20 Miles |

The 48,000 acre (19,420 hectare) Alaska Chilkat Bald Eagle Preserve is the site of the largest concentration of bald eagles in the world.

FROM FJORD *to* PHILISOPHICAL FIGHT *to* FESTIVAL

The Story of the Alaska Chilkat Bald Eagle Preserve

Bald eagles use a variety of vocalizations to communicate. Described as a combination of chirp and whistle, bald eagle vocalizations have not been thoroughly studied and are little understood.

In the Alaska Chilkat Bald Eagle Preserve, one can stand along the shores of a pristine river and watch hundreds upon hundreds of bald eagles. It's the largest gathering of these magnificent birds on earth. The combination of wildlife, rivers, valleys, mountains, and glaciers is spectacular and breathtaking.

A unique combination of natural and human forces created what is now known as the Alaska Chilkat Bald Eagle Preserve. Sections of the Chilkat River remain ice-free even in the most frigid winter temperatures. As an adaptation to this unique hydrologic phenomenon, an unusually large and late run of salmon spawns in these ice-free waters from November into January. Every year, bald eagles migrate from hundreds of miles away to take advantage of this late-season food source. Where the eagles gather is also the traditional home of the Chilkat tribe of the Tlingit people. The Chilkats have lived for centuries in harmony with the land and the eagles. As new settlers arrived and industrial-scale development threatened the eagles, a broad spectrum of people worked together to set aside and protect this unique area. Conflicts continue and new chapters are being written.

Natural History

Bordering Southeast Alaska are mountains shrouded in moisture coming off the Pacific Ocean. As the moisture hits the mountains, heavy snowfall results. Year after year, more snow falls than melts away in the summer, and the snowpack gets deeper. When the snow reaches a critical depth, tremendous pressure forces the ice crystals near the bottom

Ice falls off the Davidson Glacier. Just as rivers form waterfalls when they drop over steep terrain, glaciers form icefalls as they drop down steep terrain.

Glaciers past and present shaped the Chilkat Valley and continue to shape the preserve. The Alaska Chilkat Bald Eagle Preserve sits between Glacier Bay and the Juneau Icefield, two vast areas where ice dominates the landscape. This is how the preserve may have looked during the last Ice Age.

to change their molecular structure, creating glacial ice. Glacial ice "flows" under the force of gravity. During the last Ice Age, extremely cold weather and high levels of precipitation formed huge glaciers. Following the paths of weakness in the earth's crust known as fault lines, the glaciers carved out huge valleys. As the valleys got deeper, the mountains got steeper. One of these valleys surrounded by steep mountains is known today as the Chilkat Valley.

After the last Ice Age ended and the giant glaciers receded, rivers replaced the glaciers. Pyramid Island, at the mouth of the Chilkat River, was the toe of a giant glacier approximately 11,000 years ago.

The Tsirku, Klehini, Kelsall, and Chilkat Rivers flow through the eagle preserve. Huge glaciers mostly hidden from roadside viewers feed these rivers. From a small plane one can see how much ice still surrounds the valley.

The glaciers leave their signature on the river. From above, river channels look like braided hair. A braided river is one sign that the river's source is a glacier. Another glacial signature is the gray or cloudy color of the river water caused by suspended sediment called "glacial flour." These same rivers run clear in the winter and spring when the glaciers are no longer melting.

In the heart of the preserve, the Chilkat, Klehini, and Tsirku Rivers come together. This is where thousands of eagles can be seen in November. Gathered together with their white heads and dark bodies, they appear as politicians of yesteryear with their powdered wigs and black robes, assembled to discuss important affairs of state. For this reason, this place is called the Bald Eagle Preserve Council Grounds.

These rivers carry huge amounts of gravel and sediment from the mountains. As the steepness of the valley floor decreases, the rivers drop the material they are carrying onto the valley floor. These rivers have been dropping this material for thousands of years, and the resulting gravel beds have accumulated to tremendous depths. Measurements in the Bald Eagle Preserve Council Grounds have determined that the gravel beneath these rivers reaches a depth of 200–800 feet (60–130 meters) below the river's surface.

The space between the gravel is filled with water. In essence, the river water on top of the gravel's surface could be compared to the "tip of the iceberg." There is a huge amount of water moving underneath and between the gravel below, particularly in the area known as the Tsirku fan or Tsirku delta.

LEFT *Since fish are the mainstay of their diet, bald eagles are always found near water—either salt or fresh. This eagle sits on a rock in the Chilkoot River.*

OPPOSITE *Nataga Creek flows into the Kelsall River just upstream of the Kelsall's confluence with the Chilkat River. As winter approaches, upstream glaciers stop melting and the Kelsall River turns from a cloudy gray to an emerald green.*

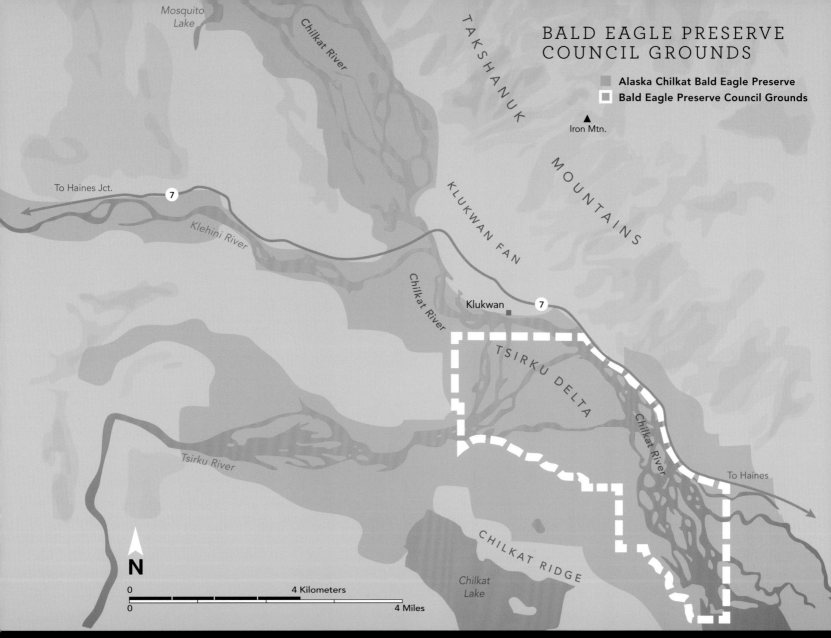

BALD EAGLE PRESERVE COUNCIL GROUNDS

■ Alaska Chilkat Bald Eagle Preserve
☐ Bald Eagle Preserve Council Grounds

Mosquito Lake

Chilkat River

TAKSHANUK

Iron Mtn. ▲

MOUNTAINS

To Haines Jct.

7

Klehini River

KLUKWAN FAN

Chilkat River

Klukwan

7

TSIRKU DELTA

Chilkat River

To Haines

Tsirku River

CHILKAT RIDGE

Chilkat Lake

N

0 — 4 Kilometers
0 — 4 Miles

This map shows the Council Grounds, the main area of congregation for the Chilkat eagles. This ice-free section of river hosts a large run of chum salmon in November.

The Tsirku River ends in an alluvial fan, a half-moon shaped deposit of sediment left by the river as it slows down. The vast amounts of sediment deposited on the Tsirku Delta, if unimpeded, would push the Chilkat River toward the village of Klukwan. But on the other side of the river, the giant Klukwan fan pushes the Chilkat River toward the Tsirku Delta. The Klukwan fan is a colluvial fan formed from giant rocks falling off the face of Iron Mountain. Even though the term "fan" is used for both the Tsirku and Klukwan fans, different processes form each one.

Over time, an equilibrium has been established. The Tsirku Delta pushes into the Chilkat River, and the Chilkat River erodes the delta as it forms. At the same time, Iron Mountain continues to erode and the Klukwan fan pushes into the river, but the Chilkat River erodes it. The Chilkat River channel, pinched from both sides, is very narrow. In military terms, you could say the Chilkat River at this point is experiencing a giant "pincer" movement, effectively squeezed from two sides. All the water flowing down the upper Chilkat, Kelsall, and Klehini Valleys is forced into this narrow channel. In the winter, deep, narrow, fast-flowing channels are the last to freeze.

The water moving under the Tsirku Delta eventually surfaces downstream, west of Klukwan. When this underwater aquifer hits the Chilkat River, the water is forced up to the surface. A variety of factors including pressure, friction, and geothermal and solar heating keeps this water from freezing. The gravel bed serves as an insulating blanket for the water trapped underneath. The upwelling water maintains a temperature of 42 degrees F (6 degrees C) year-round, well above freezing.

The combination of these unfrozen upwellings coming off the Tsirku River with the deep and fast water flowing down the Chilkat between the Tsirku and Klukwan fans is a recipe for ice-free water year-round. Even when surface air temperatures drop well below freezing, this section of river water does not freeze. In years when the ambient temperature drops to extreme low temperatures, much of the river freezes, and eagles congregate in this ice-free zone. Other years, when

A fresh layer of snow highlights each branch of alder and cottonwood trees along the Chilkat River.

the ambient temperatures are not very cold, the eagles spread out over a much larger area along the Chilkat River.

After the end of the last Ice Age, the Chilkat Valley was effectively devoid of life. The glaciers had scoured the valley to the bedrock. Years ago, college students were taught it takes a long time for plant life to establish itself after glaciers retreat. It was believed that lichens grew on bare rocks, and broke down the rocks over hundreds of years to form the soil that provides sustenance for plants to colonize. Researchers in nearby Glacier Bay National Park, however, have proved otherwise.

Over a period of twenty years, they have seen plant succession in action. At the base of the Reid Glacier, which is retreating, areas that had been covered in ice two decades ago now support flowering plants. Instead of struggling to take over recently uncovered ground, plant life becomes established with relative ease.

One catalyst for this rapid transformation is the river that flows from the toe of the glacier. Rivers move fine sediments and gravels, the basis for soil. Rivers issuing from glaciers are extremely dynamic. They erode, sort, and deposit sediments, and eventually abandon their channels, leaving some areas high and dry. Once the area is dry, pioneering algae, mosses, and plants capable of surviving in low-nitrogen soils move in. This sets the stage for gravel bar pioneer plants, like yellow dryas, to become established. These plants stabilize the gravel bars, and as they grow and die, they become soil that supports trees like cottonwood, spruce, and alder.

One of the rules of natural history is that a process one can witness today is the same process that took place in the past and will also take place in the future. The same processes taking place in Glacier Bay today occurred long ago in the Bald Eagle Preserve Council Grounds. The glaciers scoured the valley, and then rivers eroded, transported, and deposited materials along the valley floor. As the river abandoned certain sections of the valley, colonizing plants moved in. Eventually, three types of forests took over.

The first type of forest to become established after glaciation was the mixed birch and pine forest. There are still remnants of this forest along the slopes of the Takshanuk Range and Iron Mountain. While birch make for some pretty fall colors in October, eagles prefer cottonwood and spruce forests situated closer to the river and the salmon.

The most important type of forest for eagles in the preserve is the black cottonwood forest. Cottonwoods require vast amounts of water and are found along large rivers. One unusual characteristic of the black cottonwood is an ability to survive inundation by river water and gravel flows. A cottonwood tree buried in 10 feet (3 meters) of gravel after a landslide may lose its leaves and appear dead, but a few years later it can sprout a new system of roots and stems directly out of its trunk. These trees have evolved along these dynamic river systems and have adapted to these periodic disturbances. The cottonwood trees in the Chilkat Valley are huge: a world record black cottonwood, measuring 60 feet (20 meters) across its crown, was recorded along the Klehini River.

OPPOSITE *Bear Island, at the intersection of the Tsirku and Chilkat Rivers, is a favorite spot for eagles to perch and roost in November. Just below these cottonwood trees, the river stays open, and chum salmon spawn and die.*

RIGHT *The first few years of life for eagles are difficult. Only one in ten eaglets that leave the nest in September will survive the five years required to attain adult plumage.*

Cottonwoods are very important for bald eagles in the preserve all year round. In the summer, large numbers of bald eagles nest in them. In the winter, bald eagles perch by the hundreds in the cottonwoods along the Chilkat River.

Next comes the mixed Sitka spruce and Western hemlock forest. These forests are found on the higher ground along the river valley. They can't tolerate the riverside fluctuations like the black cottonwoods, but they are important for eagle survival in the winter. While cottonwoods lose their leaves in winter, spruce and hemlock trees retain their needles. When huge winter storms come in and cottonwood trees cannot provide adequate protection, bald eagles move to the spruce and hemlock forests for shelter.

Over time, after forests became established along the rivers, salmon and other fish species colonized the Chilkat. The sections of the Chilkat River that remain ice-free would be nothing but a geologic side-story were they not paired with a late run of salmon. Chum salmon typically spawn in August and September. In the Chilkat River, in the same place where unique conditions keep the river from freezing, a late and large run of chum salmon begins in November.

As salmon runs are ending all over the Pacific Northwest, British Columbia, and Southeast Alaska, the spawning season of these Chilkat chum salmon is just beginning. They start to arrive in October and hit peak numbers in November. Some fish spawn in the Chilkat River in January. Could it be that these salmon evolved to take advantage of the lack of competition for spawning beds during this late season?

Fall and winter are difficult for bald eagles. Studies have shown that nine out of ten bald eaglets that leave the nest in September will not survive the five years it takes to reach adulthood. The primary cause of death: winter starvation. Small runs of coho salmon take place all winter up and down the coast of Southeast Alaska. These runs help small numbers of bald eagles survive through the winter, but they are nothing on the scale of the Chilkat chum run. The latter numbers in the tens of thousands, and these runs are able to support thousands of bald eagles.

Facing a very difficult time of year, eagles up and down the Pacific Northwest coast and throughout Interior Alaska and Canada travel hundreds of miles to the Chilkat Valley to feed. The tens of thousands of late-spawning fish become

A mature bald eagle perches in a Sitka spruce tree. Bald eagles spend much of their time roosting and perching, keeping a lookout for salmon in the waters below.

their twenty-four-hour, all-you-can-eat buffet, open when all the other restaurants are closing down. Eagles travel from as far away as Portland, Oregon, for this feast, a distance of more than 1,100 miles (1,770 kilometers).

Eagle migration is a bit of a natural history anomaly. Bird migration in the northern latitudes is normally associated with northward movement in the spring and a migration south in the fall. In the summer months, adult bald eagles are tied to their nesting territories and cannot travel vast distances for food, but in the winter, eagles are free to go where the food is.

The dynamics of the eagle migration to the Chilkat Valley are not completely understood, but doctoral candidate Rachel Wheat is collecting more information. She has captured a number of Chilkat eagles and fitted them with satellite transponders to track their movements. She has found that eagles come from all directions in the fall and winter months to take advantage of the Chilkat food source. Over 3,600 bald eagles have been counted at one time along the river.

Even with advanced tracking methods, many questions may never be answered. For example, do juveniles learn when and how to get to the Chilkat from the adults? Is it instinct? Or a combination of both?

One thing is certain—it would be impossible for man to re-create the unique combination of forces that brings this many eagles together in one place.

LEFT *Tim Ackerman proudly wears a jacket signifying that Tlingit pride is strong in the Chilkat Valley.*

ABOVE *Brown bear claws protrude from the top of small carved faces. These adorn a bear-fur headband that sits upon a handmade sheepskin drum. Drums are an important part of any Tlingit performance. The mallet for striking the drum is made of maple.*

OPPOSITE *Carving is part of the traditional Tlingit life. Tlingit artists carved dugout canoes and totem poles. Everyday objects like spoons and bowls were artistically and painstakingly carved. A modern carving tool, known as a Swiss gouge, sits on a totem pole being sculpted by master carver Wayne Price.*

Cultural History

The human story of the Alaska Chilkat Bald Eagle Preserve is just as important as the natural history. Alaskan Natives, the resident non-Native population, as well as "outsiders"—national and international developers and conservationists—all play a part in this story.

The term "Tlingit" is used to delineate a linguistic and cultural group of Northwest Coast Natives who live in southern Southeast Alaska and north to Yakutat. The Chilkat Tlingits are the original inhabitants of this area. The story of the preserve cannot be told without considering them. This is their home.

Archeological studies are still in their infancy, but it is believed that Native people arrived in the Chilkat Valley after the Pleistocene Ice Age, which ended 10,000 years ago. Chilkat is the broad term for northern Tlingits who came here, but there are actually two distinct groups in the Haines area: the Chilkats and the Chilkoots. They came at different times and occupied different parts of the territory. Klukwan, located at the heart of the Alaska Chilkat Bald Eagle Preserve, is the ancestral home of the Chilkat people and is considered one of the most important Tlingit Native villages in Southeast Alaska. It's also the only major Tlingit village that was established inland, away from the coast.

There are very few places along the coast where low elevation mountain passes allow relatively easy travel to the Interior of Alaska and the Yukon. The Chilkats controlled one of the most important passes, the Chilkat Pass. The Chilkoots, or L'koot people, were stewards of other passes near present-day Skagway. Trade and travel over these trails were so important, the Natives called the area now known as Haines *deishu*, meaning "end or beginning of the trail."

Klukwan is situated where four major river valleys come together, just across the river from the Bald Eagle Preserve Council Grounds. It's an ideal location for a village—with access to plenty of fish, protection from wind, and an abundant and pure water source. A critical element that brought Klukwan wealth and prestige was its proximity to the Interior for trade.

Over time, a vast trade network developed. Upon first contact with white traders, the Chilkat trading sphere extended as far north as the Yukon River and as far south as Puget Sound. A key contributor to the success of the Chilkat trade

was a type of smelt known as eulachon (sometimes spelled hooligan) and, more specifically, its oil.

When these small fish arrived in early May, the local Natives collected them by the boatloads. Traditionally, eulachon were placed in dugout canoes and allowed to "cure" for about two weeks. Hot rocks were placed in water in the canoes, heating up the fish until they gave up their oil. This oil was collected, refined, and then stored for use as a condiment and tonic.

Eulachon oil was a highly sought-after commodity, and the Chilkats became very wealthy by trading with the Natives in the Interior. Trade parties traveled north over the passes in February and March by snowshoe. Chilkats were renowned for their strength: traders commonly carried loads of 100 pounds (45 kg) or more on their backs. Trade goods

included eulachon grease, dried salmon, and herring eggs. The Chilkats returned with precious furs, copper, and beadwork supplied by their trading partners, the Southern Tutchones. These goods were traded up and down the Pacific Northwest coast via dugout canoe.

This combination of a rich natural environment, relatively mild weather, an abundance of trade goods, and control of trade routes served to make the village of Klukwan one of the wealthiest on the Pacific coast. The combination of wealth and leisure time led to a sophistication of culture, including creation of masterful artwork.

In Klukwan, artists were commissioned to carve totemic designs on the house posts holding up a clan house known as the Whale House. Photographs of these posts and other art brought fame and recognition to Klukwan and the Whale House. Unlike most totemic art that was outside in the harsh elements, these carved house posts have been indoors since they were carved and remain in good condition today. In addition to the Whale House artifacts, other cultural objects like Chilkat carvings and weavings are considered among North America's finest indigenous creations.

The first white people to come to Alaska were the Russians, seeking sea otter pelts for their beautiful, dense fur. Sea otters live in ocean kelp beds, not found around Haines. Because there were few sea otters, Russians had little reason to venture into the Chilkat area and so had minimal impact. Over time, American and English traders took over the coastal fur trade, and Western goods like rifles and wool blankets became available to the Tlingits. The Chilkats added these to the trade items they carried over the pass, and were the sole source of such goods for the Natives in the Yukon.

By the mid-1800s, the Hudson's Bay Company was working its way west across Canada, seeking beaver and other furs. In 1848, representative Robert Campbell established a trading post on the Yukon River, Fort Selkirk, planning to trade directly with the Southern Tutchones. However, the Southern Tutchones were the Chilkat's main trading partners in the Interior. Although this site was hundreds of miles away from the Chilkat Valley, the Chilkats considered it part of their exclusive trading sphere. In 1852, Chief Kohklux of Klukwan led a war party to the post and burned it to the ground. Campbell wanted to rebuild the fort and punish the Chilkats, but company officials in Montreal refused. The Chilkats were too strong and the site was too remote.

This totem pole, carved by Greg Horner and Dave Svenson, is located near the Haines cruise ship dock. This section of the pole features the carved face of a woman with a coho salmon draped over her head.

The house in the middle of this view of Klukwan is the famous Whale House. Other clan houses dating to the early 1900s stand nearby.

The only real competition to the Chilkats were the Stikine Tlingits who live near present-day Wrangell, Alaska. Like the Chilkats, they had a large eulachon run and trade routes into the Interior. In the late 1870s, the Presbyterian Church under Sheldon Jackson founded a mission and school in Wrangell. The Stikine children began learning to read and write.

The Chilkat people knew the white men were coming; they were wise enough to understand they needed tools to deal with the changing times. If the Stikines learned the white man's ways and the Chilkat didn't, the Stikines would have a competitive advantage. The Chilkats invited Presbyterian minister S. Hall Young to visit Chilkat territory.

Young and naturalist John Muir arrived in 1879, paddling from Wrangell and landing at the Chilkoot village of Yandeistakye, near the present-day Haines Airport. They traveled in October, one of the rainiest months of the year, in an open dugout canoe. When they arrived on November 4, Natives surrounded the canoe, picked it up, and carried the entire group to shore for a welcome feast. After many speeches, they invited Young back to start a mission. However, the geography of the Chilkat Valley presented a challenge regarding the location of the mission. If located at Klukwan, the Chilkats would reap the benefits and the Chilkoots would have to travel a long way to visit. Built at the Chilkoot Village at Chilkoot Lake, the mission would pose the same problem for the Chilkats. The middle ground, at Deishu, was selected. Deishu sits on a low point on the Chilkat Peninsula between the Chilkat and Chilkoot sides. Frances Electra Haines, secretary of the Presbyterian mission school board, made a personal contribution of $240,000 toward the mission effort, and the mission was named in her honor.

The development of the Haines Mission had mixed effects on the Tlingit people. In their zeal, missionaries convinced the Chilkat to abandon not only shamanism, but also many other elements of their cultural identity. Many Natives moved closer to the mission and abandoned traditional village sites. Efforts were made to assimilate Natives, and the language and traditions began to lose hold. On the positive side, the mission staff tended to the health needs of Natives and provided education in English and the ways of modern society.

Tlingit leader Tim Ackerman dons an eagle headdress, bear claw necklace, and handmade leather vest.

More change was on its way. The Chilkats, in the midst of profound cultural transformation, saw their trade monopoly diminish with the arrival of Jack Dalton—an entrepreneur, cowboy, and explorer. Dalton arrived in 1890 to explore routes to Alaska's interior. The passes near present-day Skagway were shorter but much steeper: Dalton recognized that the Chilkat Pass was the best option for packing goods into the Interior by horse. He eventually improved the Chilkat Trail and established a sort of "Pony Express," a toll road with a series of trading posts and lodges along the traditional Chilkat trading route.

The trail became known as the Dalton Trail, a safe route for moving horses and cattle from the coast to the Yukon. When word got out that miners in the Yukon faced starvation, Dalton drove an entire herd of cattle over the Chilkat Pass to Dawson City. Dalton improved the trail and did not charge Natives to use it, but the Chilkats resented his intrusion into their country. They tried at various times to kill him, but failed.

Peter C. Johnson wears his regalia for a eulachon-greeting ceremony. His hat, made of red and yellow cedar, depicts an eagle in flight. Johnson and wife Dixie enjoyed sharing their Tlingit culture with local school groups.

In 1898, gold was discovered in Porcupine Creek not far from Klukwan, and more outsiders arrived. Rather than passing through on their way to the Yukon, they stayed and a town of over 1,000 residents sprang up a few miles from Klukwan.

The Chilkats were being overrun. Construction for Fort William H. Seward began in 1902. Most sources emphasize that Fort Seward was established because of a border dispute between the United States and Canada. More recent research suggests the Fort was also a check on Chilkat power. Native Americans throughout the country had been subdued, but the Chilkats were still a powerful presence in a remote area. Ironically, the army purchased its land from the Presbyterians, who had been given the land by the Natives a little more than twenty years before.

In 1909, a wagon road was pushed from Haines to Porcupine. In 1943, the Haines Highway was completed. The Chilkats' exclusive trade route, once traveled in winter by strong men on snowshoes carrying heavy packs, is now part of a highway system connecting the Pacific coast with the interiors of Canada and Alaska. The country that took weeks to traverse now passes by in a few hours at highway speeds. This road connects to the famous Alaska Highway. The relative isolation of the pre-contact period was over. More and more people were moving to Haines.

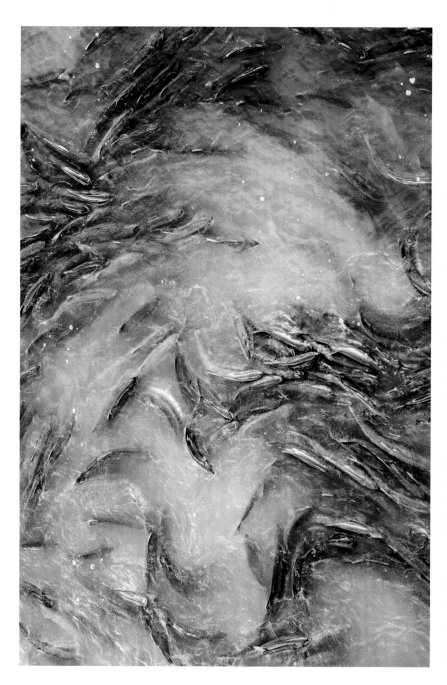

In the early 1990s, a proposal to expand the Haines Airport into the Chilkat River raised concerns about eulachon. Riverside areas were prime fishing grounds for this fish. The environmental permitting process required consultation with the local Tlingits.

Natives gathered in Haines and discussed the importance of eulachon to their culture. They described a ceremony during which the first fish to arrive were welcomed, rather than caught. "These are the scouts: they come first to let the others know how things look," explained elder Dixie Johnson. "When you go somewhere new, you want someone to welcome you, don't you? If we catch them, they may turn around and no fish will come. If we welcome them, the others will follow and there will be food for all."

As the meeting progressed, someone rushed in and shouted, "The scouts have arrived!" Caught in the excitement, they gathered at Mile 4 of the Haines Highway wearing traditional regalia and welcomed the fish with song and dance.

It became clear to the environmental consultants that Natives strongly opposed airport expansion. Their testimony was largely ignored and the expansion went ahead. To compensate for the possible disruption of their traditional fishing, an informational kiosk was built in the airport parking lot explaining the importance of this site for the Native people. Sandwiched between cars, the structure is rarely seen or used.

After the airport expansion, eulachon runs declined along the Chilkat. Fortunately, in the last few years, the eulachon have returned, arriving by the millions. Nowadays, Natives and non-Natives fish side by side for the eulachon, but only the Natives go the extra step to process the oil. To this day, eulachon oil is considered a delicacy and is an important part of the traditional Tlingit diet.

LEFT *Hundreds of pink salmon take advantage of the incoming tide to work their way upstream under the bridge along the Chilkoot River.*

OPPOSITE *An outgoing tide stranded thousands of eulachon on the mudflats near the mouth of the Chilkat River, making for an easy harvest. Millions of these smelt spawn in the Chilkat River every May.*

The Conservation Movement

Tlingits traditionally respected the eagles, seeing all creatures as separate but interdependent tribes. Eagles and ravens, in particular, were, and continue to be, deeply important to the Tlingits. The two birds make up distinct groups, or moieties, upon which Tlingit society is organized.

Western culture generally lacked this connection and understanding of eagles. Due to overfishing and the use of fish traps, salmon runs were declining by the early 1900s. Fishermen and government officials, not understanding the cause, looked for a scapegoat. Bald eagles, a healthy and vital part of the ecosystem, were blamed for the declining salmon runs and were shot by the hundreds. The attitude at the time was that the only good predator was a dead predator. Starting in 1907, the Alaska government offered a bounty for dead bald eagles.

Whitey Hakkinen had been stationed at Fort Seward in Haines in the 1940s. The territorial government was notoriously slow in paying out its bounty on eagles. One entrepreneur saw a business opportunity and became the "eagle talon broker." The broker paid fifty cents per pair of talons on the spot. When the broker amassed a large amount of talons, he sent them to the territorial government and collected double what he had paid. "Sure, I shot some eagles. That's the way it was back then," Whitey said during an educational program at the Sheldon Museum in the 1980s. The bounty on the bald eagles had little effect on the salmon runs, and was rescinded in 1952.

By the mid-1900s, bald eagles and other birds of prey in the Lower 48 states were declining from a different and unexpected cause—a pesticide known as DDT. Sprayed to fight mosquitoes, the chemical worked its way up the food chain, finding its way into fish and, eventually, bald eagles. DDT did not kill eagles directly, but it caused their eggshells to thin and crack prematurely. Bald eagles did not drop dead en masse out of the trees, but their numbers declined.

In 1962, Rachel Carson wrote her groundbreaking book *Silent Spring*. One of the first great works of the modern environmental movement, the book raised awareness of concepts like ecology, food webs, and bioaccumulation. Carson's book alerted the nation to the effects of DDT, and its use was eventually banned in the United States. The bald eagle became a national symbol of wilderness—a vital part of this story.

DDT was never used in Haines, where the bald eagle population remained strong. There were so many eagles in Haines that most locals could not appreciate that the populations of the bird were declining all over the country.

In the 1950s, exploration revealed that Iron Mountain, near Klukwan, held what was likely to be the largest iron deposit in the country. Columbia Mining Company proposed a plan to develop this deposit, divert the Chilkat River, and dispose of tailings over 3,840 acres (1,553 hectares) of floodplain. The plan was dropped in 1960 due to unprofitability.

Ravens are noted for their intelligence, while eagles are known for their strength. To the Tlingit Indians, eagles and ravens are the two most important societal subdivisions or moieties.

Just as this plan was being dropped, James King of the U.S. Fish and Wildlife Service arrived in Haines to conduct the first eagle surveys in the area.

In 1971, the Iron Mountain mining plan returned. A consent agreement was signed between Mitsubishi Corporation and the Klukwan Village Council to mine Iron Mountain. Plans were made to move the village of Klukwan, as the mining operation would cover what is today the entire Bald Eagle Preserve Council Grounds. Momentum quickly gathered against this project. The Haines Chamber of Commerce, Chilkat Snowburners, Haines Sportsmen's Association, Alaska Department of Fish and Game, and Alaska State Division of Forestry joined together to support protection of the Bald Eagle Preserve Council Grounds. The U.S. Fish and Wildlife Service recommended protecting 128,000 acres (51,000 hectares) of land.

In 1972, the state created the 4,800-acre (1,942-hectare) Chilkat River Critical Habitat Area. The Mitsubishi plan was dead. This protected the flats where the eagles gathered, but not the surrounding forest and tributary river systems critical for eagle survival.

The village of Klukwan sits on a broad outwash between the Chilkat River and the steep peaks of Iron Mountain. The mountain contains a huge deposit of magnetite, a magnetic iron ore. A proposed mine on Iron Mountain was one of the threats that led to the creation of the Alaska Chilkat Bald Eagle Preserve.

Haines by then had evolved into a logging and mill town, and money was flowing. The logging industry in Haines was in full swing in the 1970s, with Schnabel Lumber Company and Alaska Forest Products running mills and providing employment for a large percentage of the town's population. The old-growth forests seemed an inexhaustible resource.

In the late 1970s, the State of Alaska, along with the Haines, Skagway, and Klukwan communities, began developing a land-use plan for the state lands. Before 1982, state land around Haines had been largely unclassified, and a twenty-year timber sale placing most state land in the timber base was proposed. The area included prime Sitka spruce forests along the Chilkat Ridge, near the Bald Eagle Preserve Council Grounds.

The stage was set for conflict. On one side were the majority of local people, and developers interested in jobs and money from the lumber and mining industries. On the other side were those who considered the bald eagle of equal importance and were concerned about the damage industrial development would do to the birds' habitat and salmon food sources.

Though the numbers skewed toward development, some people in Haines were interested in protecting the Chilkat Ridge and Bald Eagle Preserve Council Grounds. Residents Norm and Patricia Blank, Peter and Sherrie Goll, Ray and Vivian Menaker, Dick and Julie Folta, Bruce and Gail Gilbert, and Paul Swift, among others, took an unpopular stand for conservation.

There were disputes, often heated, between the environmentalists and the pro-development residents of Haines. Tensions mounted. Ultimately, the issue was too important to be decided by a few thousand people in Haines.

The National Audubon Society came to study the Chilkat Valley to find out more about the eagles and their habitat. The society's studies showed the critical link between geology, the ice-free waters, the late salmon run, and the eagle congregation. The Audubon Society

The first snows of the season hit the Yukon Territory weeks before coming to Haines. Million Dollar Falls is a popular stop along the Haines Highway for travelers coming to visit the Alaska Chilkat Bald Eagle Preserve and Haines from the Yukon or Interior Alaska.

directed some of its research to the Chilkat Ridge, which had caught the loggers' interest. At first glance, it seemed that eagles perched in the cottonwood trees along the river, so logging nearby areas would have little effect on them. Research showed, however, that when storms with high winds and low temperatures rolled in, the eagles moved from the cottonwoods to the protection of the large spruce trees on the ridge. The studies determined that Chilkat Ridge provides vital habitat area that eagles depend on for survival.

Alaska Governor Jay Hammond took a personal interest in the eagles of the Chilkat Valley. Hammond placed a moratorium on logging until the question of habitat protection could be decided. People who worked in the mills were angry and upset with the moratorium and were motivated to come to some agreement with the conservation community. If a settlement could be reached, the moratorium would be lifted and they could get back to work.

The question of habitat protection also attracted the attention of the federal government. U.S. Senator Gary Hart of Colorado proposed making the upper Chilkat River an extension of Glacier Bay National Park as part of the Alaska National Interest Lands Conservation Act (ANILCA). This upset many locals who did not want the federal government to take control of land in the Chilkat Valley.

On one side were the federal government, the National Audubon Society, Alaska Governor Jay Hammond, and national and local conservationists. On the other side were the logging companies, the Haines chapter of the Alaska Miners' Association, and pro-development locals.

A meeting was called on January 28, 1982, where key players were brought together to sit down and draw up an agreement. Everyone had a desire to settle the matter quickly—the loggers and miners so that they could either get back to work or move on, and the environmentalists because they cared about the immediate as well as the long-term

Fierce November winds pour down from the Yukon and lift up the glacial dust deposited by the Chilkat River in the summer. Hundreds of eagles were on the flats prior to this windstorm. The next day, only a handful could be seen. The others had retreated to the protection of the spruce trees in areas like the Chilkat Ridge.

future of the eagles and fish. Heated discussions ensued but no agreement could be reached.

The meeting closed without resolution, and the various players headed to the airport. As fate would have it, a huge storm blew in as the meeting was ending, and all planes were grounded. Everyone was stuck in town until the weather cleared up.

The participants decided to sit back down and talk things over. The pressure was off—this was not a formal meeting, and no one expected to reach a resolution. Discussions progressed and continued into the early morning. At 3 A.M., a compromise resulting in the formation of the Alaska Chilkat Bald Eagle Preserve was reached.

An agreement to protect 48,000 acres (19,420 hectares) of land in the Chilkat Valley was proposed. This was ten times more land than previously protected by the 1972 agreement, but only one-third of what the U.S. Department of Fish and Wildlife had previously recommended. The agreement would protect not only the Bald Eagle Preserve Council Grounds, but also much of the Chilkat River watershed, including major sections of the Chilkat, Klehini, Tsirku, and Kelsall Rivers. Also added was the upper section of the Chilkoot River above Chilkoot Lake.

All present signed the agreement except the Klukwan village representative, who abstained. The Chilkats strongly believe that the area from the Chilkat summit to Berner's Bay, halfway to Juneau, is *Jilkaat aani*, Chilkat country. They do not readily agree to cede jurisdictional authority to any local, state, or federal agency.

A unique management entity was created. While managed by Alaska State Parks, the preserve is different from a state park. The legislation creating the preserve states that the "primary purpose for establishing the Alaska Chilkat Bald Eagle Preserve is to protect and perpetuate the Alaska Chilkat Bald Eagles and their essential habitats within the Alaska Chilkat Bald Eagle Preserve in recognition of their statewide, nationally, and internationally significant values in perpetuity." The primary mission is to perpetuate the eagles; human uses are secondary considerations.

In the fall and early winter, the Chilkat River level drops, exposing patterns in the sand created by the movement of the river water. A light snow highlights them.

Industrial logging was prohibited within the eagle preserve, as was large-scale mining. However, traditional uses such as hunting, trapping, fishing, and small-scale firewood cutting were allowed to continue. The Chilkat Ridge, so important to the bald eagles for roosting, was not included in the protected area and remains susceptible to logging.

Logging and large commercial activities prohibited in the eagle preserve are allowed in the adjacent Haines State Forest, which is managed for multiple-use.

Today, the eagle preserve's story is celebrated as a rare example of stakeholders in a resource dispute sitting down and resolving the details of lands management on their own terms. Prior to this time, policy was dictated from above. Now, such "interest-based" negotiations are a preferred method of resolving resource-use conflicts.

An eagle turns as another glides past.

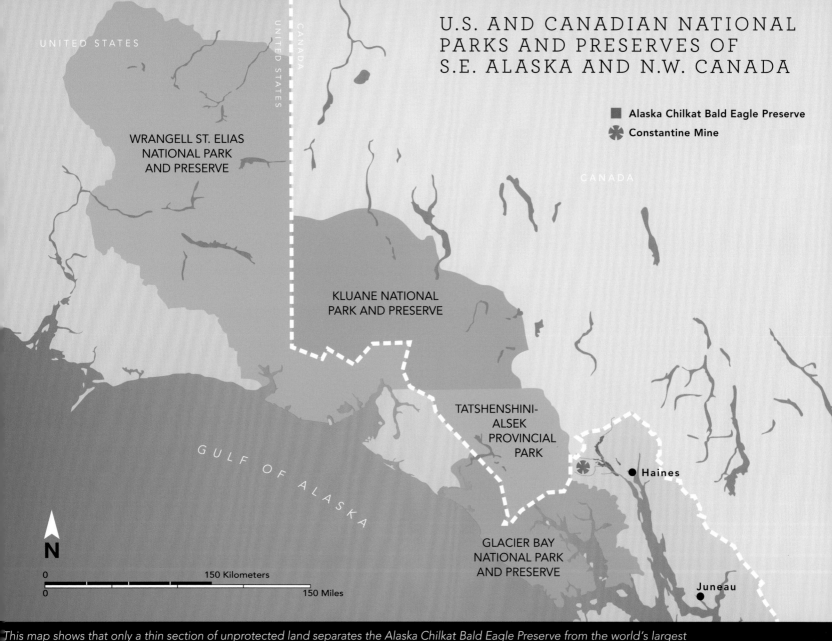

U.S. AND CANADIAN NATIONAL PARKS AND PRESERVES OF S.E. ALASKA AND N.W. CANADA

■ Alaska Chilkat Bald Eagle Preserve
✳ Constantine Mine

UNITED STATES

UNITED STATES

CANADA

CANADA

WRANGELL ST. ELIAS NATIONAL PARK AND PRESERVE

KLUANE NATIONAL PARK AND PRESERVE

TATSHENSHINI-ALSEK PROVINCIAL PARK

GULF OF ALASKA

GLACIER BAY NATIONAL PARK AND PRESERVE

● Haines

● Juneau

N

0   150 Kilometers
0   150 Miles

This map shows that only a thin section of unprotected land separates the Alaska Chilkat Bald Eagle Preserve from the world's largest protected wilderness. Unfortunately, the Constantine Mine is located just upstream from the preserve in an unprotected area.

Tourism, Conservation Conflicts, and Recent Years

At the time of the preserve's creation in 1982, Haines tourism was in its infancy. As the 1980s and 1990s progressed, a new economy arose—that of large-scale cruise ship tourism. The preserve began to draw tourists from all over the world. Tour companies offering rafting, jet boat tours, and wildlife viewing sprang up in Haines.

The fight for conservation had not ended. In the late 1980s came a proposal to open a giant copper mine along the Tatshenshini River north of Haines in British Columbia. Once again, the creation of new jobs was pitted against conservation of the environment. The Windy Craggy project proposed moving 60 million pounds (27 million kilograms) of ore through Haines for shipping. Trucks departing every eight minutes would have moved ore twenty-four hours a day over the course of fifteen years. Ore and chemicals including cyanide were to be transported through the heart of the eagle preserve on the Haines Highway.

The mine, however, promised few jobs in Haines. Also, the town had changed. With tourism promotion and publicity like the Disney movie *White Fang*, the town started attracting artists and retirees drawn by values like a clean environment and healthy lifestyle. Haines became recognized for its wildlife and scenic beauty. With the development of the Internet, people who could work remotely via computer moved to Haines for the pure water and active lifestyle. Many of the new arrivals came from places with degraded environments. They recognized the Chilkat Valley as special and wanted to live in a place where they could catch fish out of local rivers, drink the water from pure, freshwater springs, and breathe fresh, unpolluted air.

In 1993, international agencies and interest groups became involved, and the Windy Craggy project closed down when the British Columbia government declared the entire area a park. The Tatshenshini-Alsek Provincial Park, located across the border just a few miles from the eagle preserve, forms part of what is now the largest international protected area in the world, 24.3 million total acres (9 million hectares).

Tourism in the Chilkat Valley continued to expand. In 1994, the American Bald Eagle Foundation was founded, and in 1995 the Bald Eagle Festival became an annual tradition. Tourism had made its way to Haines, and at the heart of this new industry was the Alaska Chilkat Bald Eagle Preserve. The Chilkat Natives joined the tourism industry, operating a ferry system between Haines and Skagway, bringing boatloads of tourists to Haines. A new dock was built in Haines to host large cruise ships. Tourism was bringing new wealth, and new tourism taxes were advanced. By the late 1990s, four large cruise ships a week were docking in Haines.

In 2000, a darker side to industrial tourism was exposed. A Miami-based cruise company was convicted of routinely dumping dry cleaning and photo processing chemicals into the waterway in front of Haines. The company involved represented 80 percent of cruise ship dockings in Haines.

The community was divided on how to respond. Because the company represented money in many pockets, some thought Haines should remain quiet and let this issue fade. Others thought the community should actively react to this threat to pure water and healthy fish. A group of residents staged a demonstration near the cruise ship dock and handed out pamphlets to alert passengers that operators of their cruise had been involved in chemical dumping in the waters near Haines.

Exploring the valley aboard Drake Olson's Super Cub with the door open for photography provides an exhilarating and chilly November experience. The view below is of Chilkat Lake. Chilkat Ridge sits just below the lake, and the Tsirku River cuts through the snow-covered upper section of the Tsirku delta.

Val Burattin moved to Klukwan from Sicily. He and his wife, Sal, practice a traditional subsistence lifestyle. After a successful catch of sockeye salmon and an initial gutting and cleaning, Val heads out to the Chilkat River. He will return the fish heads and waste to the river before heading back to the smokehouse in the village.

After the cruise season ended, the cruise company's chief executive came to Haines to host a public meeting. Strong feelings erupted. Residents lashed out against the official for poisoning their food. Some in Haines were proud that the town had taken the corporation to task. Others were worried how the company would respond.

Soon afterward, the company announced that, due to increases in fuel prices, they would no longer dock in Haines. Haines lost 80 percent of its cruise ship dockings overnight. Rumors spread that Haines was against cruise ship tourism and did not want ships in port.

Loss of the ships hurt the local economy, but the town persevered. People in Haines want what all of us want—clean water and food that is not contaminated. History shows that if someone or something threatens these core values, Haines citizens will speak up, stand up, and fight.

The Future of the Chilkat Valley

As cruise ship tourism in Southeast Alaska reached levels of one million passengers a summer, the character of the main Southeast Alaska cruise ship ports—Ketchikan, Juneau, and Skagway—changed dramatically. Locally-owned businesses selling Alaskan arts, crafts, and jewelry were replaced by lines of jewelry stores selling diamonds, emeralds, and T-shirts.

In Haines, numbers of large cruise ship dockings dwindled to one per week. While the other ports changed drastically and quickly, Haines evolved at a slower pace. Perhaps not surprisingly, Haines began to gain a reputation as a place to escape industrial tourism. Tourists today break away from the crowds in Skagway and travel to Haines via shuttle ferry. They come in groups of 100 or so at a time. Their impact on the character of the town is minimal.

The future of Haines as a tourism destination and quality place to live is strong. Since 2000, the special nature of this community has earned it national recognition. A photo of Haines on the August 2004 cover of *Outside* magazine listed Haines as one of 20 "dream towns—the new best places to live and play." In 2005, the Gates Foundation and *Library Journal* recognized the Haines Library as the "best small library in America." Local author Heather Lende's ode to life in Haines, *If You Lived Here, I'd Know Your Name,* climbed to the *New York Times* bestseller list. The town has become a prime destination for backcountry skiing. The municipality's tourism department bills Haines as the "Adventure Capital of Alaska."

In 2009, the Haines Highway was declared a National Scenic Byway. At the thirtieth anniversary of the Alaska Chilkat Bald Eagle Preserve in 2012, Haines mayor Stephanie Scott and Klukwan leaders stood side by side extolling the virtues of the eagle preserve. The village of Klukwan is nearing completion of a museum, cultural center, and eagle observatory. For the first time, their famed artifacts will be on public display. Steve Henrikson, senior curator of collections at the Alaska State Museum, said the agreement to put the Whale House pieces on display is of international significance. "This is like a UNESCO World Heritage decision. To see art of that magnitude in its original setting is such a rare thing."

Klukwan is positioned to take advantage of increased interest in the Bald Eagle Preserve Council Grounds. The American Bald Eagle Foundation continues to expand and the Bald Eagle Festival attracts visitors from all over the world every November.

The rest of the country and the world are becoming increasingly crowded; technology is overtaking many of our lives. People are aching to find the peace and wellness that come from connecting with nature. They want to experience a place where bears come down to the rivers to feed on wild salmon while bald eagles perch above their heads. They want to meet Native people who maintain their traditional values and are proud of their heritage. They want a place where local artists create products with local materials, inspired by the boundless beauty around them. And they want to experience one of the greatest wildlife spectacles on the planet, the annual gathering of thousands of American bald eagles. Visitors can still find all this and more in Haines and Klukwan and the Alaska Chilkat Bald Eagle Preserve.

The first frost of the season stiffens grass overlooking Mosquito Lake. Before the lake freezes completely, trumpeter swans and Canada geese use the lake for resting and feeding. Soon after, they will continue their southern migrations.

History Repeats Itself

Currently there is a new threat looming—the Palmer project, a mine prospect being explored by Constantine Metal Resources. The project, locally known as the Constantine mine, is situated in the watershed of the Klehini River, just upstream of the Bald Eagle Preserve Council Grounds. According to the Constantine website: "The Constantine mine is poised to exploit a 'high grade copper-zinc rich deposit discovery with tremendous expansion potential.' This is the 'same Late Triassic volcanogenic massive sulphide (VMS) belt as the high-grade producing Greens Creek mine, and the giant 298 Mt Windy Craggy copper deposit—a world class environment.'"

The mine's developers neglect to mention that as little as five parts per billion of copper in rivers, streams, or lakes can damage a salmon's sense of smell, making juvenile salmon vulnerable to predators and disorienting adult salmon seeking home streams. They also fail to mention that the Windy Craggy project gained international attention and was halted because of its potential effect on a world-class natural area. Mine developers don't say that the Klehini River is one of the main tributaries that intersects at the Bald Eagle Preserve Council Grounds and joins with the Chilkat River directly upstream of the fall chum salmon spawning zone. Loss of that late chum salmon run would mean loss of this critical food source for the bald eagles, and the consequent loss of the eagle-gathering phenomenon.

Constantine continues: [The mine is] "located adjacent to a paved Alaska state highway, with a short (60 kilometers) haul to year-round deep-sea port facilities in Haines, Alaska, providing ready access to hungry Asian concentrate markets." There is no mention that the road they are referring to runs right through the heart of the Alaska Chilkat Bald Eagle Preserve. The stage is set for more public meetings and local conflict. Competing public relations campaigns have already started between the Constantine mine and the local conservation group, Lynn Canal Conservation. Each group has paid for ads in the local weekly, the *Chilkat Valley News*.

In August 2014, after heavy rains, British Columbia's Mount Polly mine tailings impoundment dam failed, pouring billions of gallons of mine wastewater and sludge downstream into the salmon-filled Fraser River. This event scoured salmon habitat and potentially caused long-term impacts to the salmon fishery. Photographs showed dead salmon with their skins peeling off from the toxins.

There is no technology that can guarantee a similar type of disaster would not occur upstream of the Alaska Chilkat Bald Eagle Preserve. In summer 2014, Haines experienced an unusually high number of factors, like earthquakes and record rainfall, that could adversely affect a tailings dam. The Village of Klukwan has publicly come out against the Constantine project and recently published the position paper included here on page 48.

The waters of Nataga Creek join the Kelsall River upstream of the Bald Eagle Preserve Council Grounds.

Position Paper Concerning the Proposed Constantine Mining Operation

Introduction

The Chilkat Indian Village is a Federally Recognized Tribal Government located in Klukwan, an ancient Alaska Native village positioned on the banks of the Chilkat River in Southeast Alaska. Klukwan is located twenty-two miles northwest of Haines, Alaska, and is on the Haines Highway with connections to Haines, Haines Junction, Anchorage, Fairbanks, Canada, and the Continental United States.

Issues of Concern: Disposal of Mine Tailings

Disposal of mine tailings is usually the single biggest environmental concern facing a hard rock metal mine. Toxic chemicals used to extract the valuable materials from the ore, such as the cyanide used in gold mining, remain in the tailings at the end of the process, and may leach out into ground water. Rock may naturally contain dangerous chemicals, such as arsenic and mercury, which leach into water much more readily after rock has been ground up and exposed to the wind and the rain. Acid mine drainage is the most frequent and widespread problem. Many hard rock mines (including most gold mines) extract minerals that are bound up with sulfide compounds. These compounds produce sulfuric acid on contact with air and water, a process that occurs at a very low rate in undisturbed rock, at a higher rate in unprotected waste rock (which has a large surface area and is now exposed to air), and a much higher rate in unprotected mine tailings, which have a massive surface area.

Endangering Our Traditional Way of Life

Our culture depends on the way things are connected—if the salmon or any of the natural resources are harmed, our people are harmed and the existence of our community is threatened. Our community consists of all living things. We need to protect our community to maintain our sacred balance with our traditional land-use areas. The development of the Constantine mine will present greater threats to our subsistence resources.

We also want to express the economic importance of a healthy river to the current and future generations of Klukwan. We hope to communicate to interested parties that what we are talking about is the cultural survival of our people and our traditional way of life.

Author's Note

Momentum is building in Haines to organize and express concerns regarding threats to the Alaska Chilkat Bald Eagle Preserve. For more information, contact Lynn Canal Conservation for updates and to find out how you can get involved (lynncanalconservation.org).

The residents of Klukwan are survivors. They have survived the diseases brought by the first white traders, attacks on their religion, and loss of much of their traditional homelands. They survived the breaking up of their families when their children were sent to boarding schools. At the recent groundbreaking for the Klukwan Cultural Center, Tlingit leader David Katzeek raised his hands and boomed in the Tlingit language, "This is 'Jilkaat aani' (Chilkat territory). This is our land," he declared. The village of Klukwan is fighting to preserve its culture, traditions rooted in a long history of using land without destroying it.

Chilkat elder Joe Hotch, speaking at a public meeting in Haines, once said: "We don't want the children of the next generation asking us, 'Where were you when they messed this area up? Why didn't you speak up?'"

The Alaska Chilkat Bald Eagle Preserve is too important to the creatures that inhabit it and the eagles that depend on it for its future to be decided on a local level. National and international pressure must come to bear to protect the Klehini and Chilkat watersheds. The waters of the Alaska Chilkat Bald Eagle Preserve must remain pristine so that the salmon return every fall—and with them, the thousands of bald eagles that grace this special place.

"Praise without end for the go ahead zeal
of whoever it was that invented the wheel
but never a word for the poor soul's sake that
thought ahead and invented the brake."

—HOWARD NEMEROV, POET LAUREATE OF THE U.S.
"To the Congress of the United States Entering Its Third Century," 1989

Tlingit leader Lani Hotch spearheads the quest for cultural renaissance and healing in Klukwan. Hotch wears a Ravenstail robe that she wove herself. The robe is trimmed with sea otter fur. Chilkat women were famed far and wide for their weaving skill, and Hotch keeps the tradition alive today.

During periods of extended and extreme cold, hoarfrost crystals form overnight on the frozen river margins of the Chilkat River. Steam rises off ice-free sections of water in the background.

Charles Jimmy, Sr., recognized as a "living cultural treasure," performs in full dance regalia in 1997 (left) and 2013 (right).

OPPOSITE *This U-shaped valley is located in the Chilkoot Mountains just south of Haines. Valleys carved by glaciers have a classic U shape. Valleys carved by rivers are V-shaped.*

RIGHT *A clear, spring-fed channel intersects with the gray, glacially fed waters of the Klehini River.*

Wildlife expert Mario Benassi handling a snowy owl at Kroschel's Wildlife Center. Ten species of owls live in the Chilkat Valley; most are more likely to be heard than seen.

High winds aloft blow snow off the summits of many of the peaks of the Chilkat Range south of Haines. In winter, extreme winds pummel the Haines townsite, but the Bald Eagle Preserve Council Grounds are mostly protected from these windstorms.

Pine martens, found in the spruce forest of the preserve, are the most cat-like member of the weasel family. They den in hollowed out trees. Pine martens have an acute sense of hearing that they use to help with hunting their favorite food, the red squirrel.

Moose are the most common large mammal seen in the preserve and can be found feeding on willows year-round. In winter, the plowed roads often provide the easiest route for moose to travel, so drivers must keep a keen lookout to avoid them.

The cross fox is a dark-color variant of the red fox. This fox listens intently for a vole beneath the snow, then leaps and drops down on its prey.

LEFT *The porcupine is unmistakable. Once spotted, they can be watched for fairly long periods of time, as they rely on their quills rather than speed for defense.*

ABOVE *The short-tailed weasel, or ermine, can tunnel through the snow in search of mice. With winter approaching, the ermine's fur turns white, providing natural camouflage.*

OPPOSITE *Coyotes are comfortable around human settlement and often are seen and heard along the Haines Highway and in the preserve.*

OPPOSITE *Wolves are an important predator in the Alaska Chilkat Bald Eagle Preserve. Recent studies have clarified the importance of salmon in their diet.*

ABOVE *A mink peeks its head through snow. While shy and quick, mink are one of the most common members of the weasel family to be spotted in the preserve.*

RIGHT *Lynx utilize a variety of hunting strategies, including stalking and ambush, to capture their prey. Lynx populations cycle with their favorite prey, the snowshoe hare.*

An early snowstorm dusts mountains just outside of Million Dollar Falls. A few of the aspen trees hold on to their yellow leaves.

Alpenglow paints the Chilkat Mountains a soft pink on a clear December morning.

OPPOSITE *The first ice of the year covers rocks splashed by river water. Rocks outside the splash zone are covered in frost crystals.*

RIGHT *October fog lifts off Chilkoot Lake to reveal a reflection. The Chilkoot drainage hosts an extremely productive fishery important for bald eagles' survival. The area where the upper river flows into the lake is within the confines of the Alaska Chilkat Bald Eagle Preserve.*

LEFT *A lone eagle sits on a branch in the cottonwood forest. A few birch trees provide contrast to this monochromatic scene.*

OPPOSITE *The Takshanuk Mountain Range is reflected in a clear pool along the Chilkat River.*

BOTTOM LEFT *A western toad peeks out from the foliage. This is one of the few amphibians that can be found in the preserve. With its porous skin, the western toad is sometimes called a "canary in a coalmine," as declining numbers can indicate environmental degradation.*

ABOVE LEFT *The thick bill of the raven is one way to distinguish the raven from the thinner-billed crow. In Tlingit lore, Raven created the world.*

ABOVE RIGHT *A smooth piece of driftwood shines in the spring runoff. May's spring snowmelt increases the flow of many creeks and rivers.*

OPPOSITE *The elusive wolverine is a true symbol of wilderness. Wolverines roam huge territories and are known to traverse mountain peaks, glaciers, and ice fields. They have a highly developed sense of smell and can find mountain goats that have been buried by avalanches. Opportunistic feeders, they can take down a full-grown moose wallowing in snow.*

A few freshly formed hoarfrost crystals punctuate the sunrise on the Chilkat River.

Stella Ordóñez admires eulachon as they swirl and spawn in the Chilkoot River.

OPPOSITE *Four trumpeter swans, two adults and two juveniles, land in the Bald Eagle Preserve Council Grounds. The swans take advantage of the ice-free waters to eat spawned-out salmon.*

TOP *Trumpeter swans are North America's heaviest waterfowl. Because they are about three times heavier than bald eagles, it takes a bit of effort and time for the birds to take off.*

RIGHT *A lone trumpeter swan swims in a last ice-free section of Mosquito Lake. The day after this photo was taken, the lake froze and the swan moved on.*

TOP *The elusive goshawk is adapted to fly and turn quickly through trees in pursuit of songbirds and the goshawk's favorite prey, the snowshoe hare.*

BOTTOM *While eagles prefer fish, red-tailed hawks search for small mammals like mice and voles. On warm summer days, small numbers of red-tailed hawks can be seen soaring with the eagles.*

OPPOSITE *Sometimes known as "Spanish moss," this plant is neither Spanish nor moss. It is an epiphytic lichen, a combination of fungus and algae that can live on tree branches where there is no soil. This photo is taken along Mosquito Lake Road in a muskeg, a type of bog found throughout the preserve.*

OPPOSITE *The eyes of the wolf are unmistakable. Wolves are hunted and trapped in the preserve, yet the howl of the wolf can still be heard.*

RIGHT *Lynx are rarely sighted in the Chilkat Valley, but they are known to reside in the preserve. Thickly furred feet allow them to quietly traverse snow-covered terrain.*

ABOVE LEFT *A spawned-out chum salmon nears its last breath along the shores of the Chilkat River. It won't be long before an eagle pulls the fish out and begins to feed.*

ABOVE RIGHT *Sockeye salmon are called "reds" because of their bright color during the spawning season. Here, the backs of two male sockeyes break the water as they vie for an opportunity to spawn.*

OPPOSITE *In late summer, brown bears can reliably be seen fishing for pink salmon along the lower stretches of the Chilkoot River.*

Two eagles in aerial battle. An eagle on the ground with a fish is an easy target for other eagles. Consequently, an eagle will eat a fish until its weight is reduced enough to be carried to a more protected perch. Once it takes off other eagles may pursue, causing the eagle with the fish to drop its catch.

Mantling, a type of body language an eagle uses to guard its food while eating, prevents serious confrontation. As the bird fills up with salmon, the intensity of the mantling decreases. Another eagle may read this as a signal that the time has come to displace the bird from its catch.

OPPOSITE *The magpie has striking plumage. The magpie's quick, erratic flight allows it to take advantage if a distracted eagle fails to guard a salmon carcass.*

ABOVE LEFT *An immature bald eagle looks up, preparing to defend its catch from other eagles.*

ABOVE RIGHT *This eagle has the black head and bill typical of a first-year bird. Plumage patterns change as bald eagles mature.*

LEFT *A pair of adult eagles in a spruce tree. At five years, eagles take on adult plumage: a distinctive white head and tail feathers. When mated adult eagles perch together, it is often possible to tell the sexes apart. Females are larger and can weigh up to a third more than males.*

ABOVE *An eagle looks down as it prepares to dive. Bald eagles in the preserve rarely dive down to pull swimming fish out of the river. Instead, they look for other eagles feeding on fish and dive down to steal the fish. Perhaps this is why Ben Franklin described the eagle as a bird with "bad moral character."*

OPPOSITE *Bald eagles are masters of flight. Their feathers make flight possible and provide insulation, protection, and plumage coloration. One study counted 7,192 feathers on a single bald eagle.*

OPPOSITE *Gulls arrive in large numbers to take advantage of the spawned-out salmon found along the banks of the Chilkoot River in September.*

RIGHT *A huge group of gulls feeding on eulachon takes flight along the Taiya River. Eulachon ecology is not completely understood. Tlingit tradition holds that these smelt are very sensitive to any disturbance, and will change spawning locations when stressed. In May 2015, the eulachon runs along the Chilkat and Chilkoot Rivers were weak, but the run along the Taiya River near Skagway was the largest in forty years. The run brought gulls by the thousands, as well as large groups of sea lions and seals.*

ABOVE LEFT *Eulachon are sometimes known as "candlefish" because they are full of oil. It is said that one can light the tail of a dried fish and it will burn.*

ABOVE RIGHT *Wild blueberries are one of the sixteen types of edible berries found in the Chilkat Valley.*

OPPOSITE *Brown bear close-up.*

ABOVE LEFT *The classic Roman nose of the black bear distinguishes it from the brown bear, which has a more dish-shaped face.*

RIGHT *A black bear looks up after feeding on insects. Bears' vision is similar to humans, but their sense of smell is far superior.*

ABOVE LEFT *The wolverine, with its sharp teeth and strong jaws, has a reputation as a fierce predator.*

ABOVE RIGHT *Porcupines have a variable diet. They enjoy plants, roots, tree bark, and berries, including the highbush cranberry shown here.*

OPPOSITE *The Cathedral Peaks catch an incoming storm.*

ABOVE LEFT *The Arctic tern is designed for long-distance flight. Arctic terns have the world record for migration, traveling from the Arctic to the Antarctic each year. Calculations show that the average Arctic tern flies three times the distance between the Earth and the moon during its lifetime.*

ABOVE RIGHT *Arctic terns exhibit ritualized courtship behavior, as seen in the following series of photos.*

OPPOSITE *Bald eagles spend much of their time quietly perched on branches.*

RIGHT *Eagles decorate the cottonwood trees on the western shore of the Chilkat River.*

Wilderness guide Mike Speaks looks out over the Juneau Icefield. The Chilkat Valley is located between two huge expanses of ice: the Juneau Icefield and Glacier Bay's Brady Icefield.

A lone moose uses the open river flats for travel. High winds on the river flats tend to blow the snow away. This, combined with the lack of vegetation, makes traveling on the flats easy compared to wallowing through deep snow in the dense forest.

LEFT Water runs down a moss-covered slope in late autumn on Porcupine Road. Moss and water are signatures of a rain forest. The Alaska Chilkat Bald Eagle Preserve is located in the Pacific Northwest coast temperate rain forest.

OPPOSITE LEFT Wild irises awaken in the spring and reach for the sun.

OPPOSITE RIGHT Ferns unfurl in the shape of a fiddlehead. Like most wild edible greens, fiddleheads are harvested in the spring.

LEFT *Elaborate costumes have always been part of traditional Tlingit dance performances. In the old days, dances sometimes went on for weeks during the winter months. Here, a wolf mask and pelt hang from an old wooden door.*

OPPOSITE *Cold temperatures and bright, low-angle sunlight combine to form this optical phenomenon called a perihelion.*

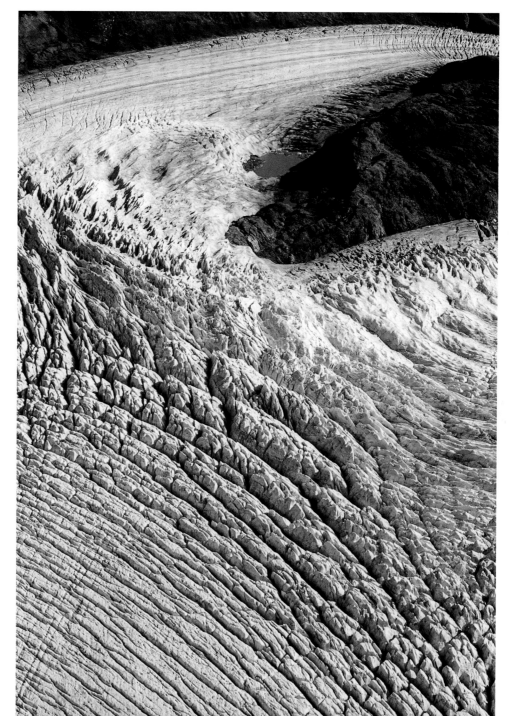

OPPOSITE *Winter storms blow snow off the ridges of the Chilkat Mountains. This aerial view looks down the Lynn Canal from just south of the mouth of the Chilkat River.*

RIGHT *The lower reaches of glacial ice are elastic and flow under the force of gravity, but the upper layers are relatively brittle. The resulting crevasses, as seen in this aerial view, open and close in response to changes in pressure.*

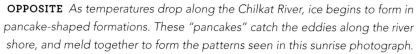

OPPOSITE *As temperatures drop along the Chilkat River, ice begins to form in pancake-shaped formations. These "pancakes" catch the eddies along the river shore, and meld together to form the patterns seen in this sunrise photograph.*

ABOVE LEFT *In early winter, the umbel of the cow parsnip maintains its integrity even after the seeds have blown away.*

RIGHT *Fall and winter seasons intermix in the Yukon. Here, an aspen tree's yellow leaves are covered by the first snow of the season.*

LEFT *An eagle perches on a branch while the sun goes down. Days are short in November and December; the sun sets behind the mountains by 2 or 3 p.m.*

ABOVE *A bald eagle calls out as another long night begins.*

OPPOSITE *Moonrise over the Chilkoot Mountains.*

BOTTOM LEFT *Eagles are fairly heavy birds (up to 13 lb/8 kg) and it can take some effort before one gets sufficient lift to take off from deep snow. This sometimes leaves a print of an eagle's feathers, including head, wings, and tail.*

ABOVE LEFT *A tattered fin of a spawned-out chum salmon pokes through the ice along the Chilkat River in November.*

ABOVE RIGHT *Mink are particularly fond of rivers, and their tracks often are seen in mud and snow along the banks of the Chilkat River.*

OPPOSITE *Looking downriver on a November morning, this is an aerial view of the Chilkat River just south of the Bald Eagle Preserve Council Grounds.*

OPPOSITE *Located a few miles south of Haines, the Letnikof Cove Cannery reflects changes in Haines' history and economy. At one time, Haines had nine canneries.*

ABOVE *The sharp beak and talons of the bald eagle are perfectly designed for catching and eating fish.*

RIGHT *After an overnight snowstorm, an eagle kicks up some fresh snow while landing.*

OPPOSITE *The Alaska Bald Eagle Festival has been a November tradition since 1995. The festival features educational presentations and daily transport to the Bald Eagle Preserve Council Grounds.*

LEFT *Young Parker Schnabel shows off some of the gold taken from his family's claim. Small-scale mines, like the Big Nugget Mine in Porcupine, have operated upstream of the preserve for years with no discernible effect on salmon runs. It remains to be decided if it is worth the risk to the salmon, the eagles, and the local economy to allow large-scale mining upstream of the Alaska Chilkat Bald Eagle Preserve.*

RIGHT *A smiling Logan Hotch dances during the groundbreaking ceremony for the Jilkaat Kwáan Heritage Center in Klukwan. Tlingit leader Jan Hill looks on from behind.*

PHOTOGRAPHING BALD EAGLES

At first glance, taking photographs of bald eagles in the preserve may seem easy, particularly in the fall and early winter when there are thousands of eagles to choose from. However, getting exceptional and memorable shots of eagles takes time, patience, and skill. The following tips are for photographers. Basic tips, like those that have to do with composition and equipment, are geared toward beginners. Most of the other comments are geared toward intermediate and advanced photographers.

Composition

There are no hard-and-fast rules for composition; these are merely suggestions. Take photos that please your aesthetic sense. Look at what other photographers have done and see what you like. Then learn to visualize what you are after, and hone your skills so that you can shoot what is in your mind's eye. Most importantly, look at your photographs after you have taken them and ask yourself what you like or do not like about a particular image. Then go out in the field, remembering what you felt, and try to improve.

Be sure your photograph has a clear and identifiable subject. The viewer should never have to guess what the photograph is about. Pay attention to the light; there is often amazing light in the Chilkat Valley. Dramatic light can change an unimpressive shot into a memorable one.

Pay attention to the background of your images. Unusually bright or dark elements in the background can distract from an otherwise great photograph. Be sure to shoot images vertically as well as horizontally. Utilize varying apertures and shutter speeds for a variety of effects.

Eventually, you will develop your own style as an artist. Enjoy the process of becoming a photographer and never let your lack of technique get in the way of savoring the natural spectacles you are witnessing. Enjoy the journey!

The mottled plumage pattern of a two-year-old bald eagle is distinctive.

Equipment

This is not an exhaustive discussion of eagle photography equipment, but rather a few tips to consider.

Lenses: Many professional photographers use 500mm and 600mm lenses. There are pros and cons to using these larger lenses. The advantage is that they can catch action far across the river that the smaller lenses can't. The downside is that they are expensive, heavy, and bulky. They require a tripod and a specialized tripod head. These lenses will have too much magnification when eagles are in close. But if you can afford to rent or buy a long lens, by all means bring one with you. Just be sure you know how to use it and feel comfortable with it before you arrive.

Don't feel like you have to spend thousands of dollars on lenses to get good shots. Remember, "It's not the violin, it's the violinist!" But if you want to invest in some high quality lenses, the Nikon 200-400 f4 VR, the Nikon 80-400, and the Canon 100-400 or equivalent are considered to be excellent lenses for eagle photography. They are light enough to be handheld and can be adjusted as eagles fly closer to and farther away from the photographer.

Tele-extenders can expand the reach of the lens, but tend to slow down autofocus capabilities. They work for portrait shots, but are not the best option for flight shots.

Camera bodies: Camera bodies with full-frame sensors provide great detail. Images can be cropped and magnified in post-production. Alternately, camera bodies with cropped sensors (Nikon is typically 1.5x and Canon 1.6x) will extend the reach of your lens. For example, a 300mm lens on a Nikon cropped sensor will turn your lens into a 450mm equivalent (300mm x 1.5).

Memory cards: Be sure to use memory cards with high write speeds (to keep the buffer from filling too quickly).

Flash: Some photographers like to use flash to get a "catch light" in the eye. The "Better Beamer" can be used to extend the reach of the flash.

Tripod: A high-quality tripod and head are critical investments. You may want to consider a monopod, as well.

An adult bald eagle prepares to flee while another eagle flies in. While eagles constantly battle over fish, injury is rare.

Clothing: Depending on the time of year, you should be prepared for anything from rain and snow to brilliant sunshine and extremely cold weather. Warm boots, warm clothes, and waterproofing for you and your camera gear are essential.

Getting the Perfect Shot: Portrait, Flight, and Battle Photography

This section deals with three types of eagle photography in order of increasing difficulty: portrait, flight, and battle shots.

Portrait Shots

What to look for: Check the eye. Most importantly, the eye must be in focus. Eagles have a second eyelid and when it is lowered, the eye looks cloudy. Like any portrait shoot, your model is important. Choose an eagle that has beautiful feathers. Adult eagles will likely be your preferred subjects when you first arrive. Once you have plenty of beautiful adult eagle shots, consider documenting the plumage variations of the juveniles. Always be aware of the light. Portrait photographs of the same bird will look different as light conditions change.

Settings: Use single-shot focus. If there are branches in the way, go to manual focus to make sure the eagle is tack sharp. Determining the correct exposure can be challenging. Adult eagles are mostly black with a white head and tail. This presents a wide range of contrast that must be taken into account. There are subtle details and variations in the darker feathers that will be lost if you underexpose your photograph. If you overexpose, the feathers in the

head will be "blown out" and you will not be able to recover any details in post-processing. One technique that works well is to enable the "highlights" or "blinkies" feature on your LCD, shoot "aperture priority," and take a test shot. If the head blinks, back off with your exposure compensation until the head stops blinking. If the head does not blink, increase your exposure compensation until the head barely starts blinking. This will give you maximum detail in the darker regions of the plumage without sacrificing the feathers on the head.

Equipment: Portrait shots are best taken using a tripod. Tele-extenders can be used with good results.

Composition: Try to get eye level with the eagle, as images of eagles looking down at you from high in a tree are rarely appealing. Look for places where the road is above the river flats; eagles perched high in trees there can be viewed at eye level from the road. When taking a picture of an eagle in a tree, be aware of branches appearing to jut out of the head of the eagle or crossing in front of the body plane. Full-frame shots of eagles are great, but you should also include "habitat" shots. Show an eagle or group of eagles as one element in a complex ecosystem including forests, rivers, and mountains with dynamic changes of light and weather.

The beauty of the bald eagle's plumage is apparent in this close-up photograph.

Flight Shots

What to look for: When you see an eagle flying toward you, focus on the bird in the center of the frame. Keep the buffer capacity of your camera in mind when you are shooting in continuous release mode. Best results are obtained when the eagle with outstretched wings fills one-third or more of the frame, with no body parts outside the frame. Keep the eagle in the center of the frame to maintain focus; you can crop for more interesting composition during post-processing. Once you have taken your first good flight shots, pay extra attention to the background and work to get a crisp shot of an eagle with the stunning mountain scenery behind it.

Settings: Because of the need for a fast shutter speed, your best bet is to wait for sunny days for your flight shots and stick with portrait and habitat shots on cloudy days. But you may not have the luxury of waiting for the weather to turn. In low light, it is better to sacrifice digital noise by choosing high ISO as opposed to utilizing a slow shutter speed. Keep shutter speed at 1/800 of a second or faster, unless you intentionally want blur on the wings. Many newer cameras can tolerate ISO of 1600 or more, so get to know your camera and find out what is the maximum ISO acceptable for your desired output (e.g., large print, web viewing, etc.). Also, practice with post-production noise reduction to see where your maximum limits are. Typically, you should stop down your aperture to f7.1 or more for flight shots.

Make sure you are on continuous focus, high-burst shutter mode, fast shutter speed, center point spot focus, and center-weighted metering. You may want to program these settings in the "presets" on your camera so that you can switch to "flight shot" mode at a moment's notice.

Equipment: If your lens is not too heavy or bulky, flight shots can be taken handheld. This is where a fast shutter speed becomes critical. If you have a large lens, you should use a tripod for flight shots. Practice tracking a flying bird with your camera on the tripod. A Wimberly (gimble-style) tripod head makes capturing flight shots easier.

Practice: When a bald eagle flies in front of you, you must have the skills to capture it in flight. Practice at home with other birds before arriving in Haines. Learn to track birds with your camera, keeping the bird in the center of the frame. Practice, shoot, and then review to see if you kept the bird in the center of the frame with good focus.

An eagle casts a strong shadow on the river flats during a bright, sunny summer day.

Battle Shots

What to look for: First, scan the riverbanks and look for an eagle eating a fish. Once you find one, set up your equipment and get ready for some action. Make sure you have all your settings correct. Shoot some test shots and check your histogram to make sure the eagle is properly exposed and in focus. Try to predict the behavior of the other eagles as they come in to steal the fish.

Settings: For battle shots, stop down to f8 or more for a wider depth of field. You will have more than one eagle and they will most likely be on different planes of focus. As with flight shots, utilizing a small aperture can present challenges in low light conditions.

Two adult bald eagles battle over a salmon along the Chilkat River.

More Tips

Cold Weather

Bring a plastic garbage bag or buy a specialized bag for bringing your camera indoors after a cold day out shooting. Before bringing the camera inside a heated room, take out the memory card and battery, and put the camera in the bag. This will prevent condensation from forming on your camera.

Study

Learn as much as you can about eagle behavior prior to going out in the field. Learn to appreciate and anticipate eagle behavior. Don't forget the other creatures in the preserve, including other birds, fish, and mammals. Pine martens, moose, river otters, ermine, mink, and even wolves and wolverines can be spotted. Bear are seen into December, taking advantage of the late salmon run. Trees, plants, berries, and geologic features all are part of the story.

Organizing Your Photos

After spending some time at the preserve, you'll likely have thousands of images to sort through, so staying organized is a must. Adobe Lightroom is a professional-level program recommended for editing, storing, and sharing your photographs.

Workshops

Attending a photography workshop and/or hiring a knowledgeable local photography guide are two ways to increase your chances of success. Rainbow Glacier Adventures LLC (RGA) offers private photography guiding in Haines year round. The best months for photographing large numbers of bald eagles are October, November, and December, but there are always eagles to be found in Haines. RGA also works closely with Steve Kroschel Films and can arrange private photography tours to his Wildlife Center. The center features wolves, lynx, wolverines, and other creatures of Alaska in natural settings where they can be photographed at close range. For lodging, RGA offers rental cabins in the heart of the Alaska Chilkat Bald Eagle Preserve. Contact Rainbow Glacier Adventures LLC for more details: info@tourhaines.com; toll free: (877) 766.3516; local: (907) 766.3576.

Afterword

My Connection with the Alaska Chilkat Bald Eagle Preserve

I first came to Alaska in the summer of 1983, fresh out of college. I traveled all over the state, worked in Denali National Park as a backcountry guide, rafted the Eagle River outside Anchorage, and worked in salmon canneries in Kenai and on Kodiak Island. Eventually, I traveled overland to Skagway, where I finished the summer washing buses and pouring coffee. While there, I remember seeing a poster of Haines with a photograph of the Chilkat Mountains gleaming behind the white buildings of Fort Seward. From the moment I first saw that photograph, I was drawn to Haines.

Three years later I returned to Alaska, working as a naturalist on an eighty-passenger expedition ship. We docked in a variety of ports in Southeast Alaska—Haines, my favorite, stood out from the rest. Part of my job was to join guests on their shore excursions, including rafting the Alaska Chilkat Bald Eagle Preserve. On my first trip down the Chilkat River, in the heart of the preserve, we floated directly underneath a pair of bald eagles perched silently in a cottonwood tree. I felt privileged to be there.

I had studied environmental education at Western Washington University, and though I was working in my field as an on-board naturalist, the shipboard life did not completely agree with me. I wanted to be outside, immersed in the wilderness. On the cruise ship dock in Haines, I met the owner of our rafting excursion, Bart Henderson. Bart was tall, rugged-looking, and exuded confidence. He was a legend in the outdoor adventure world and a pioneering international rafting guide.

Bart pointed to the mountains west of Haines. "See those mountains?" he said with a half-smile. "Glacier Bay is on the other side. Next week, a group of us will kayak in Glacier Bay for three days. We'll leave the kayaks behind, put on crampons, and climb over those mountains. Next, we'll hike down the glaciers and, where the river comes out of the ice, we'll have some rafts waiting for us. From there, we'll run the river back here to Haines."

"I want to do that," I said.

"You should," Bart shot back. It was a conversation that changed the course of my life.

When I left Alaska, I could not stop thinking about Haines, the Chilkat River, and the preserve. I sailed with the ship to Tahiti, and though the blue, tropical waters and warm breezes were enticing, I knew in my heart that I had to return to Haines. In February 1987, I

The author, center, heads north in 1988 for his first season managing river trips in the Alaska Chilkat Bald Eagle Preserve. Joining him for the 2,100-mile (3,300-km) drive north that year were guides Lorin Hayden, right, and Lee Wilhelm, left.

told Bart I wanted to work for him. Five months later, I had moved to Haines full-time and was managing Chilkat Guides and its bald eagle preserve rafting program.

In 1986, Haines had just started to promote itself as a tourism destination. With my experience on the ships, I knew that cruise ship passengers were looking for knowledgeable guides. I launched into a study of the Alaska Chilkat Bald Eagle Preserve, its natural history, the indigenous culture, and the politics that were playing out in the Chilkat Valley. That journey continues to this day. This book is the culmination of what I have learned.

After a few years guiding, training, and managing the rafting trips in the bald eagle preserve, I left day trips and started to guide ten-day camping and rafting excursions on the Tatshenshini and Alsek Rivers. These are pristine rivers that run through the heart of glacier country in Glacier Bay National Park. I soaked in the adventure while studying the land. I learned to identify the region's plants and birds. I noticed the seasonal changes and compared this knowledge to what I already knew about Haines and the Chilkat Valley. At the same time, I was building my own business in Haines, Rainbow Glacier Adventures, offering visitors a personalized experience with local residents as guides.

In the off-season, I traveled the world working on small cruise ships as an on-board naturalist. In 2002, I married Yvonne Granger, and a year later our first daughter, Stella, was born. My life was changing, and all the traveling and trips away from home took a backseat to staying in Haines and raising a family. I found myself spending more and more time in the Chilkat Valley in the winter, and I began to guide in the eagle preserve during the fall and winter eagle congregation. I honed my photography skills and added guided photography tours to my company portfolio. I have been fortunate to spend hours and hours observing and photographing bald eagles.

My connection with the Alaska Chilkat Bald Eagle Preserve got deeper as the years went by. In 2011, my wife and I bought land in the heart of the preserve, and are currently completing construction of our house and rental cabins. There is a bald eagle nest across the lake, sockeye salmon spawn nearby, and we even saw a black wolf from our front door!

In 2014, my journey came full circle as my company obtained a permit to guide rafting trips through the eagle preserve. I spent the summer floating the river. One of the highlights was taking my daughter's class from Klukwan School on a rafting trip down the river past the ancient village that lies at the center of the preserve.

A cottonwood tree is silhouetted by an ice pillar. This rare optical phenomena, called a perihelion, is caused when airborne ice crystals catch the low angle light at sunrise.

West Coast rivers were once so rich with spawning salmon it was said a person could cross the water walking atop the backs of salmon. Now, in most locations outside of Alaska and Canada, extreme measures are being taken to save the few fish that remain. Today, the Chilkat River runs pure and clear. Pure water is key to sustaining the salmon runs that attract eagles to the preserve. Without pure water, the runs will diminish and could even disappear as they have in other rivers.

This is my account of an area I have loved, lived in, and studied for over twenty-five years. My photographs are from the preserve and from within a 150-mile (250-km) radius of it. This book is my story of the land and its inhabitants. While I discuss the Chilkat and Chilkoot tribes, I do not claim to represent them.

The preserve cannot be fully captured by words and photographs. I remember standing at sunrise one crisp November morning, listening to the sounds of hundreds of eagles calling to one another. The air was filled with ice crystals as the sun broke through the horizon at the mouth of the Chilkat River, and the valley filled with light. A rainbow—or more accurately, an "icebow"—appeared, the sun shining through crystals of ice. Time stood still. And while I picked up my camera to capture the moment, I knew that my photograph would pale in comparison to experiencing this place in person.

The Alaska Chilkat Bald Eagle Preserve is vitally important not just for us, but also for future generations. This book is my humble attempt to capture the spirit of this place.

The area between Mile 19 and Mile 23 of the Haines Highway is known as the Bald Eagle Preserve Council Grounds. The area is aptly named; it appears as if the eagles have gathered in council to discuss important affairs of state.

Acknowledgments

Bart Henderson, Mike Speaks, and Greg Streveler have all been teachers and friends during my years training as a river guide and naturalist. Greg Streveler reviewed and advised on the natural history section. I spent a day with Senator Gary Hart and his wife, Lee, in Haines and heard firsthand about the federal government's interest in the Chilkat bald eagles and Senator Hart's role in the creation of the preserve. Daniel Henry, a scholar of Chilkat Valley history, provided insight regarding the Tlingit history. Lee Heinmiller and Mario Benassi helped with photo captions. Peter Goll assisted with the chronology of the conservation movement. Tom Lang provided inspiration and editing advice. Gershon Cohen, Ron Farrell, Scott Carey, Ben Kirkpatrick, Bruce Finnochio, David Lowrence, Heather Lende, and Carol Tuynman provided input. My friend Linda Wright helped with copy editing and photography review. I also want to thank my photography assistants Emily Weisberg and Brooke Foorman. Editor Tom Morphet's assistance was invaluable to the success of this book. Liz Heywood and Krista Kielsmeier helped with copy editing. This book was a dream that became a reality thanks to my project manager, Elizabeth Cromwell, and designer, Kate Basart. Their advice and expertise is warmly appreciated. My wife, Yvonne Granger, provided endless support and editing assistance.

I want to give special credit to my photography mentors, Oliver Klink and Ron Horn. Ron volunteered hours of his time to assist me with areas of photography that were challenging. Oliver not only instructed me in advanced photography techniques, but also served as an example of how a professional photography guide conducts himself in the field.

Resources

Jilkaat Ḵwáan Heritage Center (jilkaatkwaanheritagecenter.org)—*Cultural tours of Klukwan.*
American Bald Eagle Foundation (baldeagles.org)—*Educational institution focusing on the American Bald Eagle.*
Haines Convention and Visitor's Bureau (www.haines.ak.us)—*Provides travelers with up-to-date information about activities in Haines.*
Alaska State Parks—Alaska Chilkat Bald Eagle Preserve (dnr.alaska.gov/parks/units/eagleprv.htm)—*State agency charged with administering the Alaska Chilkat Bald Eagle Preserve.*

Travel and Tour companies

Reservations by Randa (alaskar4you.com)—*A local travel expert for tours in Haines and the preserve, hotel, travel and tour bookings.*
Rainbow Glacier Adventures LLC (tourhaines.com)—*Year-round tours in the preserve including small group rafting trips, photography tours and workshops, private tours and cabin rentals.*
Alaska Nature Tours (alaskanaturetours.net)—*Nature-oriented tours in the preserve year-round.*
Chilkat Guides Ltd. (chilkatguides.com)—*River rafting trips during the summer months.*
Chilkat River Adventures Inc. (jetboatalaska.com)—*Jet boat tours during the summer months.*
Haines Rafting Company—*River rafting during the summer months.*

Printed in China

Design and layout: Kate Basart/Union Pageworks | Project management: Elizabeth Cromwell/Books in Flight | Cartography: Ani Rucki

ISBN: 978-0-692-47733-5
Joe Ordóñez/Rainbow Glacier Adventures LLC| P.O. Box 1103 | Haines, AK 99827 | (877) 766-3516, (907) 766-3576 | www.joeordonez.com